Witchcraft Summons: Prayers for Overpowering witchcraft Summons

TABLE OF CONTENTS

CHAPTER 6   61

CHAPTER 1

The Reality

The realm of the physical typifies what happens in the realm of the spirit. So when you see certain things happening in our mortal realm, it is an indication that the reality is what happens in the realm of the spirit. The earthly court system works effectively to be able to bring offenders before it. When someone has committed a crime or a person whose presence is required before a court of law, the court issues a summons to him to appear before the court. The summons is issued by the authority of the court mandating the person whose name appeared in the summons to come before the court at a certain time or day. If that individual fails to comply with the order of the summons, he can be punished by that court that issued the summons against him. It is the attendance of that individual that determines what happens on the day that is named in the summons. The summons could say that the person is to appear before the court to answer an allegation against him or if the individual is to defend the case brought in by another person, he could be summoned to defend the case. I said earlier, it is the content of that summons that determines what will happen in the court on that day. If the summons says, appear before me, the individual has no choice but to come and put up an appearance on that day. If the summons says the person is to come and defend a particular criminal allegation against him that is what he will come and do on that day. It is the content of the summons that determines the business of the court on that day. In other words, the summons can guide the judge as to what he is required to do against the individual whose name appeared in the summons.

In the same way that it happens in the physical, that is how it happens in the realm of the spirit when witchcraft summons is issued against a person. Witches and wizards use the medium of their covens to issue summons against people that they want to cause an appearance before them. Once that summons has been issued by a witchcraft coven, the person whose name appeared in that summons must put up an appearance whether he likes it or not. Except if that individual is shielded from answering to any summons as a result of his belonging to the body of Christ or the observance of certain spiritual principles as a child of God. We will discuss these in details when we get to subsequent chapters of this book how you can refuse to answer a witchcraft summons that was issued against you. But for now, I want you to have a foundational understanding of what a summons is and how witches use witchcraft summons to compel the appearance of an individual to attack the person or destroy the life of that person that has been summoned before the coven of witches.

Friends, this is something that you need to know that while you sleep on your bed, tossing and turning in the pool of your sleep, someone may be awake trying to command your appearance before their coven so that their attack can gain expression in your life. This is the basis of witchcraft summons and what they do. There are many people whose life has been upended as a result of the fact that they answered witchcraft summons. Others were not so lucky who weren't protected by the covering of the blood of Jesus, maybe dead now as a result of the attack of witchcraft summons. One of the things you can always do as a believer is to prevent yourself from answering to a witchcraft summons because once you do and before their coven, it is only the mercy of God that can protect you from the deadly attack of that witchcraft coven. I am not trying to scare you, it is the reality that I am trying to paint before you so that you can know what to do whenever a witchcraft summons has been issued against your life. And this is what the subject of this book will be to help you understand properly what witchcraft summons do and how to prevent it from working against your life. The Bible tells us in the book of Hosea, that my people perish for lack of knowledge. So if a person does not have a level of understanding of spiritual things, those things can work against his life and sometimes as a result of ignorance he may die. May that never be your portion in the name of Jesus. It is for this reason that we dare to take up some of the most neglected subjects in the Christian faith to open the eyes of the believer to the realities of these things and how they can use their weapons of warfare to destroy them. The Bible tells us that the weapons of our warfare are not carnal but mighty through God to the pulling down of strongholds (2 Corinthians 4:10). One of such weapons we will employ in this book is the weapon of prayer.

Friends, whenever it is time for you to lift your voice in prayer towards the end of the pages of this book, I want you to pray as you have never prayed before in your life so that any witchcraft summons that was issued against you or the life of your family can be destroyed through the power of the prayers you are going to offer. I pray that the Lord will bring speedy deliverance to you as you begin to pray the prayers in this book in the name of Jesus.

CHAPTER 2

Is it in the Bible?

This is one of the first issues that we need to resolve. If what we are preaching and teaching does not have the basis of the word of God, then you should never accept it. I will show you an example of how a witchcraft summons was used in the Bible and demonstrate to you that it has a basis in the word of God. Saul was one of the anointed Kings of Israel that God chose to govern his people. He started very well by executing the commandments of the Lord with all his heart. But as time progresses, pride sets in and Saul began to do what he pleased. He chose what commandment to obey and the one he does not need to obey. He sank deeper into the funnel of disobedience until one day when the Lord decided to shut him out of all answers. The Bible tells us that when war was imminent upon the Israelites, all the channels by which Saul was used to hearing the voice of God were closed.

1 Samuel 28:6

> *And when Saul inquired of the Lord, the Lord answered him not, neither by dreams nor by Urim, nor by prophets.*

God refused to speak to him by dreams, by the prophets or even by Urim. The situation got so worse that Saul did not know what to do. And the man he had been relying on to hear the voice of the Lord had died, Prophet Samuel. To hear the voice of the Lord, Saul had to devise a means, and one of the things he did was consult a witch at Endor. The scripture I'm about to quote is a pretty long reading but patiently read it.

1 Samuel 28:7-14

> *7 Then said Saul unto his servants, Seek me a woman that hath a familiar spirit, that I may go to her, and inquire of her. And his servants said to him, Behold, there is a woman that hath a familiar spirit at Endor.*
> *8 And Saul disguised himself, and put on other raiment, and he went, and two men with him, and they came to the woman by night: and he said, I pray thee, divine unto me by the familiar spirit, and bring me him up, whom I shall name unto thee.*
> *9 And the woman said unto him, Behold, thou knowest what Saul hath done, how he hath cut off those that have familiar spirits, and the wizards, out of the land:*

wherefore then layest thou a snare for my life, to cause me to die?

10 And Saul sware to her by the Lord, saying, As the Lord liveth, there shall no punishment happen to thee for this thing.

11 Then said the woman, Whom shall I bring up unto thee? And he said, Bring me up Samuel.

2 And when the woman saw Samuel, she cried with a loud voice: and the woman spake to Saul, saying, Why hast thou deceived me? for thou art Saul.

13 And the king said unto her, Be not afraid: for what sawest thou? And the woman said unto Saul, I saw gods ascending out of the earth.

14 And he said unto her, What form is he of? And she said, An old man cometh up; and he is covered with a mantle. And Saul perceived that it was Samuel, and he

stooped with his face to the ground, and bowed himself.

15 And Samuel said to Saul, Why hast thou disquieted me, to bring me up? And Saul answered, I am sore distressed; for the Philistines make war against me, and God is departed from me, and answereth me no more, neither by prophets, nor by dreams: therefore I have called thee, that thou mayest make known unto me what I shall do.

16 Then said Samuel, Wherefore then dost thou ask of me, seeing the Lord is departed from thee, and is become thine enemy?

17 And the Lord hath done to him, as he spake by me: for the Lord hath rent the kingdom out of thine hand, and given it to thy neighbour, even to David:

18 Because thou obeyedst not the voice of the Lord, nor executedst his fierce wrath upon Amalek,

therefore hath the Lord done this thing unto thee this day.

19 Moreover the Lord will also deliver Israel with thee into the hand of the Philistines: and to morrow shalt thou and thy sons be with me: the Lord also shall deliver the host of Israel into the hand of the Philistines.

He intended that when that which has spoken to him, he would be able to know what to do concerning the war that was looming over the horizon of the Israelites. How sad! How can a man go to seek the counsel of the Lord from those who God has given a judgemental word, suffer the witch not to live. Saul had been one of the men that were at the forefront of cutting off all witches and wizards in the land of Israel. So any witch that hears anything about the name of Saul would tremble in trepidation because he chased them out of the land. So when Saul came on that day to consult that which at Endor, the woman was greatly shocked.

The moment she knew that Saul was the person who came to see her, she began to beg for her life. Saul assured the woman that nothing would happen to her for making consultations on his behalf. Now, this is a very interesting part of the Scripture and how it relates to witchcraft summons. When the woman asks Saul what he wanted, he said he wanted the Prophet Samuel to be summoned. When they did, Samuel appeared and gave Saul a verdict of what was going to happen to him and his entire household. The fact that they were able to call the spirit of Samuel or someone who looked like Samuel is a form of witchcraft summons. But I need to explain something very important here that someone can't summon the spirit of a saint from heaven. That is impossible. But the Scripture is very illustrative of witchcraft summons how they call the name of people in their coven and bring them up to execute their attacks.

It could be a familiar spirit that was used to talk to Saul on that day who knew of the pending judgement of the Lord hanging over the life of Saul and quickly pronounced it over him. However, the Scripture typifies a classical example of a witchcraft summons especially when the calling of the name of a person is involved. As we will see in subsequent chapters, one of the ways that witchcraft uses in summoning people to their coven is through names because the name of a person is the identity of the individual both in the realm of the spirit and in the realm of the physical. It is simple. Whenever someone calls your name, won't you answer? Of course, you will. That is the basis of a witchcraft summons; I have shown you in the Scripture under reference, it has a foundational basis in the word of God. Witchcraft did not start today. This is something that has been practiced many generations ago even during the time of Jesus Christ. Remember the activities of the life of Saul was in BC.

Now that you know that this is foundational in the word of God, I want you to read this book with an open mind trusting the Lord to be able to open your heart to the revelations that have been given here. I know that some of the things you read here may sound somehow to your understanding, but I want you to trust the Holy Spirit to guide you as to what is contained in this book. Already, we know that it is in the word of God and at least there is a basis upon which our teaching is standing.

CHAPTER 3

Witchcraft Summons You Wished You Knew

There are certain types of witchcraft summons that I want to draw your attention to so that you can know how to handle them in case someone tries to use it against you to cause you to appear before their witchcraft coven.

Wicked summons

The Bible tells us in the book of Psalms that God is angry with the wicked every day.

Psalms 7:11

> *God judgeth the righteous, and God is angry with the wicked every day.*

And as we discuss this type of summons you will begin to understand the reason why the anger of God is burning continuously against all wicked men and women. The Bible tells us in the book of Exodus that suffer the witch not to live. When reading the pages of that chapter of the Bible, the first thing that will come to the mind of many people is that God is too harsh against witchcraft. But as you will soon see, witches employ the use of their coven to issue wicked summons against people to destroy their lives. It is for this reason that God will judge all wicked men and women especially those who indulge themselves in witchcraft activities. And I will show you precisely how this witchcraft summons works. A wicked witchcraft summons has no basis upon which it was issued. I want you to pay close attention to what I am about to teach you. When a wicked witchcraft summons has been issued against an individual, it was issued purely based on an evil intent and wickedness. That means the individual has done nothing wrong to warrant the issuance of that witchcraft summons against his life. Even if the person has done something wrong, witchcraft is not the recognisable way to solve differences among humans. It was purely out of wickedness that this summons was given against the person. Sadly, the majority of the people who answer to witchcraft summons fall into this category. You did nothing to that uncle of yours. You did nothing wrong to that cousin of yours. You did nothing to that neighbour of yours, but he decided to use a witchcraft summons against your life, not only a witchcraft summons but a wicked one at that. What did you do to deserve that kind of summons against your life? Your answer is as good as mine, you did nothing wrong. This is why this type of summons is called wicked witchcraft summons. So when you see God making a pronouncement against witchcraft it is not because he wants them to be dead. In reality, God desires to have souls saved and for them to make it to eternity on the last day. The Bible tells us clearly that hell was made for the devil and his angels. However, if a man decides to partner with the devil through the medium of witchcraft, it is the punishment meant for witches that he will get. It is for this reason that God said, suffer the witch not to live. In essence, the spiritual punishment for witchcraft that God has placed is capital punishment – the sentence of death. And when you are praying the prayers in this book I want you to be fully aware that the judgement of God can fall in this manner against witchcraft practitioners who have been using wicked summons against your life. In case you have a loved one engaging in witchcraft activities, and you don't want the judgement of God to come against that person, the best way to pray is to add the element of mercy to your prayer. God, you know I love this person so much, but he has been using witchcraft summons against my life. I pray that you will show this person mercy but if he refuses to repent, let the full weight of your judgement against witchcraft come upon him now in the name of Jesus.

Whenever you see yourself in dreams gathering before a group of people, and they are acting as if they are judging you, then you should know that that is a sign that you are under the direct influence of a wicked witchcraft summons. When you hear a name being called especially when you are about to sleep, a wicked witchcraft summons may have been issued against you. And they are making all efforts to ensure your appearance before them so that your life could be subject to their attacks. The witches know that it is only when they can compel your appearance before them that they can do whatever they please with your life. When a person is too powerful to answer a witchcraft summons, what they can do is to shoot arrows against a person's life. But if that witchcraft coven can successfully issue a wicked witchcraft summons against your life, and you appear before them, they can do whatever they want to do with you. Which is the reason why one of the highest means of attack of witches is through the medium of wicked witchcraft summons. It is just like a man has been bound hand and foot and handed over to you to do whatever you please with him. In the same manner that the Philistines had Samson, their mortal enemy bound with his eyes plucked off and vulnerable to any kind of attack that they throw against him that is how witchcraft summons works when a person appears before them. It was issued out of pure wickedness and the reason why the witchcraft summons was directed at the person is for the destruction of his life.

Friends, the matter of witchcraft summons must not be handled with kid gloves. It must be handled with all forms of seriousness in the place of prayer to have it destroyed and broken.

Basis Witchcraft Summons

2 Corinthians 10:4

> *(For the weapons of our warfare are not carnal, but mighty through God to the pulling down of strong holds;)*

I quoted the above Scripture for a particular reason. In the same way that the weapons of our warfare are not carnal but mighty through God for the pulling down of strongholds that is the same way that the basis witchcraft summons is to witches. Please don't get confused, I'm going to explain all that I'm saying to you. Basis witchcraft summons is whenever you have a problem with anyone who is engaged in the practice of witchcraft. He goes into the witchcraft coven report you before that coven and requires that a witchcraft summons be issued against your life. The reason why this is done is that you will be compelled to appear before that coven as a result of the issuance of that summons which bears your name so that you can answer the allegation that has been reported against you in that witchcraft coven. The person that reported you will also be among those who will issue that basis witchcraft summons against you. Once you have appeared before that coven, they will speak to you and whether you can answer it or not, your attacks start from there. I want you to recall when you had a problem with someone, and the person warned you that you will see what he will do to you. Few days after the person warned you that you will see what I will do to you, you discovered that certain things which were not happening to you started to happen. If that person is a witch, then it is very likely that he went and reported you to their witchcraft coven, and a basis witchcraft summons was issued against you. Once that witchcraft summons was issued against you, and you answer to it based on the problem that you had with the member of that witchcraft coven, your attack begins. So the weapons of their warfare that they used against people is basis witchcraft summons, and this becomes possible whenever you have a problem with a person who is a member of the witchcraft coven. They will threaten you that I will deal with you. And that dealing that they are referring to is resorting to their witchcraft coven so that the basis witchcraft summons can be given for you to appear before them. On the day of your appearance before that witchcraft coven following the issuance of that basis witchcraft summons, they can decide whatever attack that they want for you to undergo. So whenever you have a problem with someone who you know is a witch and shortly after you begin to experience intense problems in your life, my friend, check it critically maybe you have answered to basis witchcraft summons.

Some people the moment they answer to basis witchcraft summons and a sentence of ill-health was passed against their lives, they will begin to have ill-health of unknown origin that no medical doctor or medical lab no matter how experienced can determine the source of the problem. Whenever they go for a medical test, they will be given a clean bill of health that they are doing very okay and there's nothing wrong with them. However, the person knows deep down within himself that all is not well. That is how a basis witchcraft summons work which is the reason why as a child of God you must not be unprotected because people are indeed very wicked. If you offend them, they will use whatever they can to ensure that you are brought under their attacks.

Plain Witchcraft Summons

A plain witchcraft summons is one that is issued against a person and that type of witchcraft summons has no basis for its issuance. Most of the times witches employ the use of plain witchcraft summons for the demonstration of power. They want to prove that they can bring anybody before their coven to answer to anything that they want him to answer. When a person answers to a plain witchcraft summons, what happens is that they can decide to put something on him. As I earlier said, that the world is a wicked place indeed. One passage of the Bible reads thus: let the wickedness of the wicked come to an end (Psalms 7:9).

How do you know that you have been summoned to appear before the witchcraft coven because of plain witchcraft summons? Simple. When you see yourself in dreams standing before people to be judged a plain witchcraft summons may be working against your life. Again the power of prayer and some of the tools that we will recommend you to use can prevent this type of attack from happening against your life. As a popular cliché goes, prevention is better than cure. It is better to stop the issuance of a plain witchcraft summons against your life than to come back later and be praying for God to deliver you from the attack of witchcraft that happened as a result of a plain witchcraft summons. I pray that the Lord will help all of us in the name of Jesus.

CHAPTER 3

How Witches use their Summons

I want to show you how witches use summons against your life to compel your appearance before them.

Name-calling

Name is the only cognizable way by which a person can be called. When God created Adam in the Garden of Eden, he gave him the responsibility of naming all the animals in the world. He looks at a particular animal and says, you are a lion.

Genesis 2:19

> *And out of the ground the Lord God formed every beast of the field, and every fowl of the air; and brought them unto Adam to see what he would call them: and whatsoever Adam called every living creature, that was the name thereof.*

He looks at another one and says you are a hyena, yet for another, he says you are chicken. And whatever names that Adam gave, the Bible tells us that that was the name of it. When Moses had an encounter with God in the wilderness and was doubting the possibility of being sent to the same Pharaoh he had been fleeing from, asked a very fundamental question. His question to God was, peradventure these people may ask me what is the name of the person that sent you to us. What will I tell them? The response that God gave to Moses was simple, I Am That I Am.

Everything both in heaven and on earth has a name. And it is by that name that a thing can be called. God the Father has a name, sometimes he reveals himself to man as Jehovah RAFA, El Shaddai, Elohim, Jehovah Jireh. Even in our present times, based on what the Lord has done for you, and your encounters with him, you can call him names. One common name that my countrymen in Nigeria use is, **Jehovah overdo**. The use of a name is very significant in both the affairs of the earth and eternity. When Lucifer was in heaven, his name was Lucifer one of the finest angels of God. When he fell, there was a change of his name to Satan the greatest demon that ever lived. I use the word lived because his time is short.

The son of God, Jesus has a name. The Bible tells us in the book of Philippians that at the mention of the name of Jesus every knee must bow and every tongue must confess that Jesus is Lord. That is his name and whenever you call upon the name of Jesus there is a response from eternity to mortality.

In the same way that names are called, that is the same way that witches use names as a medium for bringing people into their coven through witchcraft summons. I want you to understand that every earthly summons that is issued by a court of law, has the name of the person required to appear before it. It is that summons that will tell who is to appear before it. If a summons contains the name of John Lee, Desiree Hills can't answer that summons because it wasn't directed to her.

One of the ways that witchcraft uses to ensure that a person appears before them in answer to a summons is a name. They would call the name of the person so that he can be summoned before that witchcraft coven. For instance, if a person is answering to a wicked evil summons, the first thing you will hear is the name of the person when compelled to appear before it even though the summons is a wicked summons. So the name is very instrumental to the issuance of witchcraft summons. Without your name, you can't appear before any witchcraft coven. This is one of the primary ways by which witchcraft summons is used against the life of a person. Once his name is called in the coven as a result of a summons that was issued against the person, he will have no choice but to appear before the coven.

One of the ways to know that a witchcraft coven has been calling your name is that you will hear your name being called and whenever you turn your back to answer you will notice that no one is calling you. It is also possible for you to experience a situation where in the night you will hear your name being called and whenever you check to see who was calling you, you will see no one.

I also need to create a balance here because it is possible for God to call your name. The Bible tells us in the book of Samuel that God was calling Samuel, but he didn't know that it was God that was calling him.

1 Samuel 3:4-6

4 That the Lord called Samuel: and he answered, Here am I.
5 And he ran unto Eli, and said, Here am I; for thou calledst me. And he said, I called not; lie down again. And he went and lay down.
6 And the Lord called yet again, Samuel. And Samuel arose and went to Eli, and said, Here am I; for thou didst call me. And he answered, I called not, my son; lie down again.
7 Now Samuel did not yet know the Lord, neither was the word of the Lord yet revealed unto him.
8 And the Lord called Samuel again the third time. And he arose and went to Eli, and said, Here am I; for thou didst call me. And Eli perceived that the Lord had called the child.
9 Therefore Eli said unto Samuel, Go, lie down: and it shall be, if he call thee, that thou shalt say, Speak, Lord; for thy servant

heareth. So Samuel went and lay down in his place.

10 And the Lord came, and stood, and called as at other times, Samuel, Samuel. Then Samuel answered, Speak; for thy servant heareth.

It was only when his mentor and the prophet that God has appointed over his life guided him that Samuel knew that it was the Lord that was calling him. One of the greatest ways to know that it is God calling you is the presence of peace. The test of peace is one of the greatest ways to distinguish between what is of God and what's not. The Bible says I will listen and hear what the Lord will say to me for the Lord will speak peace.

Psalms 85:8

I will hear what God the Lord will speak: for he will speak peace unto his people, and to his saints: but let them not turn again to folly.

Anything that does not follow after peace, then you know that it is of the devil. So whenever you hear your name being called and it causes so much fear in your life, it is time to take up the mantle of prayer and destroy that witchcraft summons that is being used against your life.

Friends, it is possible that as you have read what is contained above, you begin to realise that witchcraft summons was used against your life because you heard your name been called in certain places but you took it for granted. And after that, you began to experience strange things in your life. Your finances after that kind of experience nosedived. It could be your health, that after you have heard your name being mentioned severally with no human being calling you, strange affliction settled on your life. It could be family that after that kind of attack of hearing your name being called, the peace that was once existing in your family disappeared into thin air. It is never too late to recover anything that the enemy has stolen from your life through witchcraft summons. The Bible tells us that God is a God of restoration. If the Lord can restore lost years, it is something that happens to your body or your life that he can't restore? Wipe your tears child of God because deliverance is about to come to you right now in the name of Jesus.

Invocation

This is one of the tools frequently used by witchcraft summons to compel the appearance of an individual. An invocation is a command issued to a named person to appear in response to a witchcraft summons. No invocation can ever take place without calling the name of a person. Name-calling and invocation and even witchcraft summons go hand in hand. The major difference between name-calling and invocation is that one is normally issued through a command. The person is compelled to come whether he likes it or not. When it comes to name-calling through the use of witchcraft summons, the person is called and because his name has been called in the realm of the spirit, he will normally appear since the spiritual is greater than the physical.

Witchcraft summons makes use of invocation a lot when it comes to dealing with the lives of people. And several people have been invoked to appear before certain witchcraft covens without their knowledge. And that is what you will be doing in the subsequent chapters of this book, praying to destroy all form of witchcraft summons that may have been issued against your life. We have already discussed the danger of being compelled to appear before any witchcraft coven as a result of the witchcraft summons. When you appear before them, they can do whatever they want to do with your life especially if that individual is not shielded by God or protected through the mercies of God.

Materials

It is not all the times that witchcraft summons always follows the pattern of name-calling and invocation. A summons may be issued against a person, but he does not necessarily need to be compelled to appear before it through invocation or the calling of a name. Once that witchcraft coven can have access to anything belonging to that individual, they can use it as a point of contact to compelling the appearance of that person through witchcraft summons. What do I mean? Let me explain to you what it means.

When a witchcraft coven wants to make a person appear through the use of his materials, they can decide to use the picture of that person so that there will be a point of contact between that picture in the realm of the spirit and that individual in the realm of the physical. It is through the picture that the person can be compelled to appear in answer to a witchcraft summons. This may sound weird to some people, but I can tell you that it is the reality of what happens on our earth. Several persons are careless about some of their belongings and possession and witches were able to take advantage of those things to bring them into their coven. It could even be a piece of cloth that you have or any material possessions that can sufficiently be linked to your physical body. If those witches can have access to those things, they can use it as a medium for compelling your appearance through witchcraft summons. I have heard countless stories of people whose pictures were taken to witchcraft coven for them to be attacked. Others have just a little material possession that has been attached to their body, for example, clothing. Those witches were able to use that as a medium for bringing them into their coven. Which is the reason why anything that belongs to you should be securely guarded because you do not know who your enemy is. Am I trying to put fear in you? At all, why should I do so when the Bible tells us that the Lord has not given us the spirit of fear but of a sound mind and boldness? However, the penalty for ignorance in the realm of the spirit is dead because the Bible tells us that my people perish for lack of knowledge. May that never be your portion in the name of Jesus. When we write about some of these neglected subjects in the body of Christ, it is because we want the eyes of God's people to be opened to the reality of some of these things so that they can be delivered from what the devil wants to use against them.

However, whatever material that had been taken from your life to the coven of witchcraft I pray that the fire of God be commanded at this moment to appear in it so that they will not be able to use it to make you appear before them in the name of Jesus.

Friends, nothing should be taken for granted. There was a time when one of my clothing was missing. When I spoke to one of my believer friends, he told me that whenever any of his clothes mysteriously disappears, he prays over it. Of course, I learned something very important from that brother on that day that nothing should be taken for granted because the enemy and his host of agents aren't joking about when they want to attack. We can't at this point be ignorant of the devices of the devil. How can you imagine that a piece of cloth can become a tool in the hands of witches and wizards who want to compel your appearance in answer to witchcraft summons.

CHAPTER 5

Am I Protected?

This is one of the first questions that we should answer. If a witchcraft summons has been issued against you, will it work? If the witchcraft summons is going to work, then there is something that you need to do very quickly and that is what I am going to show you in this chapter of this book.

The Cover of the Blood

One of the greatest ways to shield your life against the attack of any witchcraft summons is through the covering of the blood of Jesus.

Revelation 12:11

And they overcame him by the blood of the Lamb, and by the word of their testimony; and they loved not their lives unto the death.

The above Scripture is very clear, that we overcame the devil by the blood of the Lamb. And every witchcraft that you see today, obtained their power from the devil. If we can overcome their master, the devil through the blood of the Lamb, then those who got their powers from the devil cannot hurt us if the blood of Jesus can answer for us in all situations of life. It was the same blood of the Lamb that was slain and placed on lintels of the doorpost of the children of Israelites that serve as a protective shield from the spirit of death that was hovering over the land of Egypt. The Bible says whenever I see the blood, I will pass over you. I have never seen any witch that is witch enough to dare the blood of Jesus. If you tell any witch to go against the blood of Jesus it is like a direct death sentence upon that witch. The blood of Jesus is available for all those who are children of God. While the blood of Jesus was shade for all of mankind, but the power of the blood is available only for those who are children of God. It is part of the benefit of salvation. The Bible says that the blood of Jesus speaks better things than the blood of Abel.

Hebrews 12:24

> *24 And to Jesus the mediator of the new covenant, and to the blood of sprinkling, that speaketh better things than that of Abel.*

Witches and wizards are not only afraid of the blood of Jesus shaded on the cross of cavalry, they are also terrified by the speaking of the blood of Jesus. Whenever a believer employs the use of the blood of Jesus against witchcraft summons, the blood does not only attacks that witchcraft coven, it speaks to it also.

So when the Bible is saying that we overcame him by the blood of the Lamb, it is also saying that we overcome all witchcraft summons by the blood of the Lamb too.

Friends, pleading the blood of Jesus in the right way over witchcraft summons is one of the simplest ways to destroy the powers and nullify the effect of that summons over your life. If the blood of Jesus is correctly and rightly pleaded from the foundation of a functional relationship with the Lord, that is, being a child of God that has been redeemed by the blood, it will prevent a child of God from answering a witchcraft summons. We have said earlier that the blood of Jesus speaks better things than the blood of Abel. So whenever those witchcraft covens are trying to summon you and the blood of Jesus is at work, what they will be hearing is the voice of the blood. You can't summon this, my son or daughter. That is the power of pleading the blood of Jesus over witchcraft summons. The blood of Jesus has both preventive and destructive effect against witchcraft summons. By preventive, it serves as a means of stopping the believer from answering the calls of witchcraft summons that have been issued against his life in the realm of the spirit. By destructive, the blood of Jesus can instantly destroy that witchcraft coven and nullify the effect of that witchcraft summons. There is nothing that can be compared to the blood of Jesus when it comes to spiritual warfare whether against witchcraft or their summons. And that is what you will be doing in the prayer section of this book.

Have an Altar of fire

Whenever witches are issuing a summons against the life of anybody, they are issuing that witchcraft summons from their altar. And whenever a believer has neglected the need to have an altar of fire in his life, he has made himself very vulnerable to all the attacks that the witchcraft summons are firing against him. When we become busy for prayers, the word of the Lord and even fellowship with other believers we are living our Christian lives dangerously. Any time an arrow is shot by the kingdom of darkness, it is possible for that satanic arrow to locate us. May that never be our portion in the name of Jesus.

Friends, never neglect your prayer altar for anything at all. When you notice that the fire of your prayer altar is going down, immediately cry to the Lord for help because the strength of the power of your Christian life is dependent upon your prayer altar. Now when I speak about altars, I am referring to all type of altars including the altar of your word study, your prayer life, and your sacrifices to the Lord. These are some of the things that will answer for you in the days of trouble when a witchcraft summons has been issued against you. The Bible tells us that the Lord will remember your covenant and sacrifices and answer you in the day of trouble.

Psalms 20:1-3

> *The Lord hear thee in the day of trouble; the name of the God of Jacob defend thee;*
> *2 Send thee help from the sanctuary, and strengthen thee out of Zion;*
> *3 Remember all thy offerings, and accept thy burnt sacrifice; Selah.*

Some things will answer for you while you are sleeping, and one of those things is your altar.

Friends, whenever the devil is beginning to invite you to a life of prayerlessness by giving you an excuse that you are very busy now, or giving you an excuse why you should stay away from the word of God, it is an invitation to destruction. A prayerful Christian is a powerful Christian. And a powerful altar will produce a very dangerous Christian that can become a terror to any witchcraft coven that wants to issue any form of summons against him. I pray that the Lord will give us the grace to maintain a prayerful altar in the name of Jesus.

The Cover of his Name

The Bible tells us that the name of the Lord is a strong tower the righteous run onto it and they are safe (Proverbs 18:10). There is nothing that offers protection against the work of witchcraft summons like the name of Jesus. Whether it is the name that you want to use to destroy an evil summons that has been issued to command your appearance, or you want to make use of the name of Jesus to prevent a futuristic attack of a witchcraft summons, the name of Jesus is the safest route for doing so. This is very important especially when you are confronted by a witchcraft threat. If a witch threatens you, and from your observation, you have seen that there is a possibility that an individual can use a witchcraft summons against you;

pray in the name of Jesus and scatter all that the person wants to do against you. It is also possible to go into the place of prayer and keep calling the name of Jesus because the Bible tells us that at the mention of the name of Jesus every knee must bow. I want to show you something about the coven of witchcraft and all the practitioners in that coven, that is, the witches that they all have a knee. Everything that bows to the name of Jesus, has a knee. The Bible tells us that when we mention the name of Jesus all knees must bow and every tongue confess that Jesus is Lord. So the name of Jesus is a weapon that is made available to the believer for a time like this – destroying all witchcraft summons.

In the place of prayer, you can keep mentioning the name of Jesus repeatedly for hours that is a weapon for battle. That is also a plan for spiritual warfare because when you mentioned that name, a lot of things happen in the realm of the spirit. Witchcraft coven crumbles and all the works of darkness are destroyed. That is the power in the name of Jesus which is available to all of us through the sacrifices of the blood of Jesus that was made on the Cross of Calvary.

Friends, as you prepare to pray I want you to understand that one of the ways to destroy the works of witchcraft coven is through the instrumentality of the name of Jesus. And I pray today that as we employ the name of Jesus for the destruction of all witchcraft altars and their summonses, it will produce results for us in the name of Jesus.

God's Jealousy

Provoking the jealousy of God is not something that can be achieved in one day, it is a lifestyle that the believer needs to follow before he can provoke the jealousy of God over his life. I can tell you that one of the fearsome dimension of the judgement of God comes from his jealousy. Pharaoh was buried in the red sea as a result of the jealousy of God over his worship of his people. Let my people go that they may serve me. A believer who can live in such a way that the jealousy of God is provoked, he is the one that will enjoy protection from all forms of arrows that come from the kingdom of darkness. You cannot live the way you want and still be able to provoke the jealousy of God.

Abraham was such a man that was addicted to the lifestyle of obedience to the extent that God regarded his life of obedience as a point of friendship. If you look at the book of James, Abraham was regarded as a friend of God.

James 2:23

> *And the scripture was fulfilled which saith, Abraham believed God, and it was imputed unto him for righteousness: and he was called the Friend of God.*

He had a very dogged commitment to the life of prayer because the Bible tells us in the book of Genesis 19:27:

And Abraham gat up early in the morning to the place where he stood before the Lord:

And because of the way he lived his life, he was able to provoke the jealousy of God. When Abraham went to Egypt Abimelech saw how beautiful Sarah was and decided to take her.

Genesis 20:1-7

And Abraham journeyed from thence toward the south country, and dwelled between Kadesh and Shur, and sojourned in Gerar.
2 And Abraham said of Sarah his wife, She is my sister: and Abimelech king of Gerar sent, and took Sarah.
3 But God came to Abimelech in a dream by night, and said to him, Behold, thou art but a dead man, for the woman which thou hast taken; for she is a man's wife.

4 But Abimelech had not come near her: and he said, Lord, wilt thou slay also a righteous nation?
5 Said he not unto me, She is my sister? and she, even she herself said, He is my brother: in the integrity of my heart and innocency of my hands have I done this.
6 And God said unto him in a dream, Yea, I know that thou didst this in the integrity of thy heart; for I also withheld thee from sinning against me: therefore suffered I thee not to touch her.
7 Now therefore restore the man his wife; for he is a prophet, and he shall pray for thee, and thou shalt live: and if thou restore her not, know thou that thou shalt surely die, thou, and all that are thine.

But while Abimelech was sleeping, God came to him in the dream of the night and told him that you are a dead man because he has taken the wife of a man that I have a lot of jealousy over. I want you to understand something very important from the Scripture under reference that it's possible that Abimelech had been taking the wives of other people before. But when he decided to try a man over whose life the jealousy of God hangs, he got a sentence of death. Abimelech had to beg God for his life in that encounter of the night. He was then given another chance to go and make the immediate restoration of the woman that he has taken.

When Pharaoh also attempted to take away the wife of Abraham by force, the Lord plagued Pharaoh and his entire household greatly.

Genesis 12:14-20

> *14 And it came to pass, that, when Abram was come into Egypt, the*

Egyptians beheld the woman that she was very fair.

15 The princes also of Pharaoh saw her, and commended her before Pharaoh: and the woman was taken into Pharaoh's house.

16 And he entreated Abram well for her sake: and he had sheep, and oxen, and he asses, and menservants, and maidservants, and she asses, and camels.

17 And the Lord plagued Pharaoh and his house with great plagues because of Sarai Abram's wife.

18 And Pharaoh called Abram, and said, What is this that thou hast done unto me? why didst thou not tell me that she was thy wife?

19 Why saidst thou, She is my sister? so I might have taken her to me to wife: now therefore behold thy wife, take her, and go thy way.

20 And Pharaoh commanded his men concerning him: and they sent him away, and his wife, and all that he had.

Why did Abraham enjoy such type of protection from God? The answer is simple, the way that Abraham lived his life he was able to provoke the jealousy of God. That is one of the important things that you need to know for God to be greatly jealous over the life of a man, it is your lifestyle that will provoke it. Many people's wife has been collected but when it came to the wife of Abraham, Abimelech got the shock of his life. Why? He was playing with a man that has the jealousy of God over his life.

I need to create the balance here, while the protection of God is available to all of God's children, there are certain fearsome dimensions of the protection of God that is only given to those who have been able to provoke the jealousy of God. Some of us who are children of God have no time for prayer, whenever the Lord gives us any instruction we cherry-pick which one we want to obey; the one that does not favour us we discard it.

Friends, if we can live the Abrahamic life, we will be able to see the Abrahamic results. We can't live the way we want and expect the jealousy of God to be provoked over our lives. If we want to see a certain fearsome dimension of the protection of God and his anger over our enemies, then there is a way to live. A life of total dedication to God can easily provoke his jealousy. Look at how dedicated Abraham was to God. He had a very rigid prayer time with God that nothing could disturb. He was waking up every morning to go and spend time with God. This was a dedication to the lifestyle of prayer. And as Abraham lived that way, God was very jealous over his life.

Friends, if you can provoke the jealousy of God no witchcraft summons can ever work against you no matter how potent that witchcraft coven is. The moment they try to invoke your name, it is fire from God that shall proceed from his throne. While you are sleeping on your bed, fire is going out from the presence of the Lord and consuming all of your enemies. This is what happens when the jealousy of God is upon your life there are certain things that witchcraft coven cannot do against you because when they try, they will be judged by the fire of God. The Bible tells us that our God is a consuming fire, and I believe that is what the coven of witchcraft are all afraid of – the consuming fire of God. But you cannot provoke the jealousy of God when you are not a man that lives according to the dictate of the Holy Spirit. The Bible tells us that the law of the spirit of life in Christ Jesus has set me free from the law of sin and death. It is whatever that the Holy Ghost tells you which is not in contradiction with the word of God that is a law. It is what should guide your life every day and when you begin to live that way full of the spirit of God, the jealousy of God will be provoked and anyone who dares your life, he is playing with grave danger. That is what the jealousy of God can do in the life of a man, and it is my earnest prayer that we will be able to lead our lives in such a way that the jealousy of God can be provoked.

Things have been made easier for us than it was in the days of Abraham as a result of the presence of the Holy Spirit in our lives. There isn't any believer on earth who does not have the Holy Ghost in him because the Bible tells us that the Holy Spirit is a seal of God's ownership over the life of every child of God. If a believer wants to live a life of dedication to God or a life that is pleasing to the Lord, he does not need to look far away. It was the same counsel that the Holy Spirit gave using the life of Moses when he said that, whatever instruction I am giving to you today is not in the mountain or the sea that you will be contemplating who will go down or go up and get it for us. It is in your heart. And who is in your heart? The Holy Ghost! The believer can never live the way God wants him to live without the Holy Ghost in his life.

No wonder those who are full of the Holy Ghost did a lot of exploits in the Bible.

I pray that God will take us to that level where we can lead lives that is so pleasing to him that his jealousy over us is provoked and whenever any witchcraft coven dare to summon us through the use of witchcraft summons, they will be surprised by the response of God in the name of Jesus.

CHAPTER 6

Prayers that destroy Witchcraft Summons

I want you to take this aspect of this book seriously and pray with passion because the Bible tells us that the fervent prayer of a righteous man avails much.

Prayer for mercy

No matter how passionate you are about destroying witchcraft summons or their attacks over your life, if you regard iniquity in your heart the Lord can't hear you. What we need to do is to ask God for cleansing through the blood of Jesus so that there is nothing that is standing between us and our maker. Once you can obtain purification through the blood of Jesus, we will pray and God will hear. This is the first prayer that we need to pray.

Reflection

1 John 1:9

> *If we confess our sins, he is faithful and just to forgive us our sins, and to cleanse us from all unrighteousness.*

Hebrew 4:16

> *Let us therefore come boldly unto the throne of grace, that we may obtain mercy, and find grace to help in time of need.*

Prayer

Holy Father, I want to thank you for the privilege of the blood of Jesus that gives me access into the holy of holies to you be all the glory and the honour in the name of Jesus.

Heavenly Father, any form of bitterness in my heart against anyone today I release them in the name of Jesus.

Gracious Father, in any area of my life that I have exulted iniquity and sin, today I come before you, and I asked for mercy in the name of Jesus.

Heavenly Father, I come before you today to ask for mercy over all the instructions that you have given me which I have failed to obey, I make demands for your never-failing mercy, and I pray that another opportunity will be given to me to obey those instructions again in the name of Jesus.

Holy Father, I make demands for the blood of Jesus to thoroughly cleanse me from every type of sin that can prevent my prayers from been answered in the name of Jesus.

Heavenly Father, you have said in your word that let us, therefore, come boldly before the throne of grace that we may obtain mercy and find help in time of need. This is the time that I require your mercy so that my prayers can go before your throne and return as answers in the name of Jesus.

Glorious Father, anything that can serve as a hindrance to the effectiveness of my prayer today, I pray that it should be removed in the name of Jesus.

Holy Father, by the speaking of the blood of Jesus that speaks better things than the blood of Abel, I make demands on the blood to speak mercy on my behalf as I go into the throne of grace for the destruction of all witchcraft attacks against my life in the name of Jesus.

Thank you, Righteous Father, for hearing and answering my prayers to you be all the glory and the honour in the name of Jesus.

Inviting the Holy Spirit

One of the sweetest ways to pray is to have the Holy Spirit invited as an expert leader. The Bible tells us in the book of Romans that the Holy Spirit will make intercession for us with groanings that cannot be comprehended by any mortal man. So the Holy Spirit will be able to come into that prayer if you can invite him the only thing that you need to do is to extend that invitation.

Reflection

John 16:13

> *Howbeit when he, the Spirit of truth, is come, he will guide you into all truth: for he shall not speak of himself; but whatsoever he shall hear, that shall he speak: and he will shew you things to come.*

Romans 8:26

> *Likewise the Spirit also helpeth our infirmities: for we know not what we should pray for as we ought: but the Spirit itself maketh intercession for us with groanings which cannot be uttered.*

Prayer

Holy Father, I invite the Holy Spirit into this prayer right now in the name of Jesus.

Righteous Father, I pray that as the Holy Spirit comes into this prayer at this moment, he will take total control of the prayer from the beginning to the end in the name of Jesus.

Gracious Father, I make demands that the presence of the Holy Spirit will make a difference in this prayer that I am praying against witchcraft summons in the name of Jesus.

Holy Father, you have said in your word that the Holy Spirit will make intercession for us I pray that the Holy Spirit can make intercession for me in this prayer for the destruction of witchcraft summons in the name of Jesus.

Holy Father, I pray that the Holy Spirit will strengthen me to pray as I ought to in the name of Jesus.

Gracious Father, I pray that as the Holy Spirit comes into the arena of my prayer against witchcraft summons at this hour, I pray that he will release his fire into my prayer in the name of Jesus.

Holy Father, anything that can prevent the working of the holy spirit in this prayer, I pray that let it be removed in the name of Jesus.

Gracious Father, let the power of the Holy Spirit be made manifest throughout this prayer from the beginning till the end in the name of Jesus.

Thank You, Holy Father, for hearing and answering my prayer because I know that the Holy Spirit is right here with me so that this prayer can destroy all witchcraft activities or works including witchcraft summons against my life in the name of Jesus.

My Name with fire prayer

This is a type of prayer you pray when there is a threat over your life by a witch, and you know that the person can make use of witchcraft summons against your life. In this type of prayer, you ask the Lord that your name be clothed with his fire so that whenever your name is called it is the fire that shall respond to that witchcraft coven. If the mention of the name of Jesus causes the release of fire, then your name can also provoke the release of fire because the Bible says you are joint-heirs with Christ. And the reason why Jesus came to the earth and died on the cross of cavalry is so that we can be conformed to the image of Christ. It is the pleasure of God for us to be His representative on earth and take charge of the works of darkness. The Bible tells us that little children that it is the pleasure of the father to give us the kingdom.

Reflection

Zechariah 2:5

> *For I, saith the Lord, will be unto her a wall of fire round about, and will be the glory in the midst of her.*

Hebrews 12:29

> *For our God is a consuming fire.*

Prayer

Lord, I want to thank you for the opportunity given to me to present my petition before your throne of grace at this hour let your holy name be glorified in the name of Jesus.

Heavenly Father, I make demands right now that you clothe my name with fire in the name of Jesus.

Holy Father, whenever my name is mentioned in any witchcraft coven as a result of the issuance of the witchcraft summons against my life, I pray that let my name provoke the release of judgemental fire against that witchcraft coven in the name of Jesus.

Gracious Father, in the same way, that the name of Jesus can provoke the release of fire since you have said in your word that we are joint-heirs with Christ, today I make demands that my name too as your son or daughter will provoke the release of fire whenever it is called in any witchcraft coven in the name of Jesus.

Holy Father, I pray that you will attach a level of judgemental fire to the calling of my name in any witchcraft coven as a result of witchcraft summons in the name of Jesus.

Heavenly Father, I pray that you will cause a release of terror on my name so that whenever it is called in any witchcraft coven because they want to summon me, I pray that your fire will answer in the name of Jesus.

Holy Father, I pray that from today henceforth my name (mention your name) will carry a dimension of your fearsome fire against all witchcraft activities in the name of Jesus.

Thank you, Holy Father, because I am fully aware right now that my name has been clothed and covered with your fire so that whenever it is called as a result of any witchcraft summons, that name will do great destruction to the works of witchcraft in the name of Jesus.

The Name of Jesus that answers by fire prayer

While the first prayer we have prayed above deals with your name to answer to any witchcraft summons with fire, this particular prayer deals with every type of evil summons so that whenever your name is mentioned in any witchcraft coven it is the name of Jesus that will answer for you. We have already discussed the power of the name of Jesus in the previous chapter, and it will be needless for us to talk about it again. Well, the Scripture says that at the mention of the name of Jesus every knee must bow and every tongue confess that Jesus is Lord. And the name of Jesus is a strong tower every righteous man that runs to it shall be saved.

Reflection

Philippians 2:10-11

> That at the name of Jesus every knee should bow, of things in heaven, and things in earth, and things under the earth;
> And that every tongue should confess that Jesus Christ is Lord, to the glory of God the Father.

Proverbs 18:10

> *The name of the Lord is a strong tower: the righteous runneth into it, and is safe.*

Prayer

Heavenly Father, thank you for the privilege I have been given to come before your throne and make my petitions to you. Let your holy name be glorified in the name of Jesus.

Holy Father, where ever my name is being called in any witchcraft coven I pray that the name of Jesus will answer for me in the name of Jesus.

Glorious Father, the same fearsome dimension that the name of Jesus carries so that whenever it is mentioned all knees bow in heaven and on earth that Jesus is Lord, let that name begin to answer to every witchcraft summons issued against my life in the name of Jesus.

Heavenly Father, the exchange that happened on the cross of cavalry is so that Jesus can take the place of my death and I can take the place of his life. I pray that let that exchange happen for me whenever my name is mentioned in any witchcraft coven as a result of a witchcraft summons in the name of Jesus.

Glorious Father, you have said in your word in the book of Hebrews that my God is a consuming fire. I make demands that whenever my name is mentioned the consuming fire that is in the name of Jesus consume all witchcraft activities which may have been made as a result of a witchcraft summons in the name of Jesus.

Holy Father, I pray today that where ever my name is mentioned in the kingdom of darkness so that I would appear because they want to summon me, I pray that let the name of Jesus answer with the fearsome dimension of the judgement of God in the name of Jesus.

Gracious Father, I pray that anywhere that my name is mentioned because of witchcraft summons, let the name of Jesus answer for me with the judgement of God so that all the priest or priestess of that witchcraft coven will be cut off in the name of Jesus.

Righteous Father, you are the judge of all the earth, I pray that your judgement will always respond to any witchcraft summons whenever my name is mentioned in the name of Jesus.

Holy Father, I make demands that whenever my name is mentioned in any witchcraft coven, I pray that may they experience the full destructive weight of the name of Jesus in response of that witchcraft summons in the name of Jesus.

Gracious Father, I make demands at this hour that where ever my name is invoked as a result of any witchcraft summons, may the full power in the name of Jesus be manifested to that witchcraft coven in the name of Jesus.

Thank you, Lord, for hearing and answering all of my prayers above because I know that from now henceforth whenever my name is mentioned in any witchcraft coven it is the name of Jesus that shall answer for me in Jesus name. Amen.

Prayer for Jesus to enter Appearance

This is a very unique type of prayer that can cause Jesus to physically appear to any witchcraft summons that was issued against your life. Remember the essence of the witchcraft summons is to cause the appearance of the person named in the summons. For instance, if the person that is mention in the summons is Greg J., It is that person that will appear whenever his name is called. But remember that the cross of cavalry came to make an exchange for us so that what we couldn't do by ourselves through the empowerment of the sacrifices of the blood of Jesus on the cross of cavalry, can now be freely done. So whenever the witchcraft coven calls your name, instead of you appearing in answer to that summons, it is the master, Jesus himself that will cause an appearance to be entered on your behalf. And you can imagine what will happen to that witchcraft coven. Even if it is the kingdom of darkness with the highest level of demonic activities that issued any summons against your name, this is one of the dangerous prayers to pray so that Jesus will cause an appearance for you.

Reflection

1 John 3:8

> *He that committeth sin is of the devil; for the devil sinneth from the beginning. For this purpose the Son of God was manifested, that he might destroy the works of the devil.*

Romans 5:6

For when we were yet without strength, in due time Christ died for the ungodly.

Prayer

Thank you, Lord, for the privilege that you have given to me to come before your throne and to pray at this hour to you be all the glory and the honour in the name of Jesus.

Holy Father, I make demands that the Sun of righteousness will cause an appearance to be entered on my behalf to all witchcraft summons issued against my life right now in the name of Jesus.

Righteous Father, anywhere that my name is mentioned, let Jesus appear in-person to that witchcraft summons in the name of Jesus.

Gracious Father, whatever type of summons that may be issued against my life whether it is a plain witchcraft summons, wicked summons, or basis witchcraft summons I pray that Jesus will appear on my behalf in the name of Jesus.

Holy Father, let Jesus who is the master over the universe be my representative on all witchcraft summons that may be used against my life in the name of Jesus.

Holy Father, I pray that Jesus will substitute me in that witchcraft summons and appear on my behalf whenever my name is mentioned in that witchcraft coven in the name of Jesus.

Holy Father, I pray that the appearance of Jesus in that witchcraft summons that was issued against my life will mark the beginning of my freedom from all witchcraft activities in the name of Jesus.

Thank you, Holy Father, for hearing and answering my prayer because I know that from now henceforth anywhere that my name is mentioned in any witchcraft summons Jesus will enter an appearance on my behalf in the name of Jesus.

Prayers that Break the Shackles of witchcraft Summons

If a witchcraft summons has ever worked against your life, and you suddenly discovered that things around you have upended, you can break free from the attacks that came from that witchcraft summons. The truth is that, whenever a man has answered to the summons of witchcraft, one of the early manifestations that the summons is working against his life is domination, oppression, control, and manipulation. These are typical examples of witchcraft attacks that a person experiences. We are going to pray in case you are experiencing any of the above after an attack of witchcraft summons.

Reflection

Proverbs 6:5

> *Deliver thyself as a roe from the hand of the hunter, and as a bird from the hand of the fowler.*

Isaiah 10:27

> *And it shall come to pass in that day, that his burden shall be taken away from off thy shoulder, and his yoke from off thy neck, and the yoke shall be destroyed because of the anointing.*

Prayer

Holy Father, I want to thank you for the privilege that you have given to me to come before your throne of grace and to present my petition onto your holy name to you be all the glory and the honour in the name of Jesus.

Gracious Father, any area of my life that has been under the direct control of witchcraft attack as a result of the witchcraft summons that was issued against me today by the power in the blood of Jesus I terminate that attack in the name of Jesus.

Heavenly Father, I stand today by the authority in the name of Jesus, and I pray that any area of my life that has been under the domination of witchcraft attack, today I break free in the name of Jesus.

Righteous Father, whatever manipulative grip that this witchcraft summons has on my life, I stand today by the blood of Jesus and asked for its termination in the name of Jesus.

Holy Father, every financial sentence of lack and want that the enemy has placed upon my life as a result of this witchcraft summons today I decree that it is overturned in the name of Jesus.

Gracious Father, every sickness that these witches and wizards have decreed upon my life as a result of this witchcraft summons which was issued in my name, I return that affliction to that witchcraft coven in the name of Jesus.

Righteous Father, you have said in your word that on that day shall the burden be lifted off your shoulders because the yoke shall be destroyed as a result of the power of the anointing, I pray at this moment that by the anointing of the Holy Spirit that breaks the yoke, every yoke of witchcraft summons that has been hanging upon my life making me suffer unnecessarily today I pray for complete deliverance in the name of Jesus.

Holy Father, every member of that witchcraft coven that was responsible for the issuance of that witchcraft summons on my life I pray that let your judgemental fire come upon them now in the name of Jesus.

Gracious Father, every priest or priestess that performed a supervisory role over that witchcraft coven that is responsible for the issuance of that witchcraft summons today I pray that the priest or priestess be cut off from the face of the earth in the name of Jesus.

Holy Father, every mark that these witches have placed on my life so that certain calamities will continue to happen to me, I pray for the complete deletion of those witchcraft marks in the name of Jesus.

Holy Father, today I pray for the release of your judgemental fire upon that witchcraft coven that wants to issue or has issued any witchcraft summons against my life in the name of Jesus.

Heavenly Father, I stand today by the power in the blood of Jesus, and I nullify every witchcraft summons that has been issued against my life in the name of Jesus.

Gracious Father, whatever type of witchcraft summons that has been issued against my life so that a portal is opened for them to continue to attack me, today I shut down that witchcraft portal in the name of Jesus.

Heavenly Father, I pray for the restoration of everything that this witchcraft summons have caused me to lose by the power in the name of Jesus.

Glorious Father, any chain that this witchcraft summons has placed upon my life today I pray that these chains are broken by the power in the name of Jesus.

Thank you, Lord, for hearing and answering all of my prayers to you be all the glory and the honour in the name of Jesus.

Our Books

1.   Obtaining Restoration in the Courts of Heaven: Courtroom Prayers for All Round Restoration

2.   Witchcraft Summons: Prayers for Overpowering witchcraft Summons & Refusing to Answer their Call

3.   Monitoring Spirits: Prayers for Destroying Monitoring Spirits and Receiving Deliverance

4.   Evil Gatekeepers: Prayers to Break Free, Enter and Possess what's Yours

5.   Overthrowing Evil Altars Secrets Revealed: Prayers for Dismantling Evil Altars

6.   Praying the Blood of Jesus the Right Way: Pleading the Blood of Jesus for Turnaround

7.   Prayers that Destroy Water Spirits: Freedom from marine Kingdom and Marine Spirits

30.   30 Days with the Holy Spirit: Powerful Prayers and Devotional for Personal Connection with the Holy Spirit and Be His Friend

31.   Breaking Evil Altars: Prayers, Decrees, Declarations for Dismantling Evil Altars

32.   How to see the Supernatural: Powerful Prayers that open the Unseen Realm

33.   Breaking the Spell of Disfavour: Prayers Declarations and Decrees

34.   Deliverance from Shame and Reproach: Prayers, Declarations for Victory

35.   Prayers that Destroy Infirmities & Diseases: Powerful Prayers that bring Healing to the Sick

36.   Courtroom Prayers: Prayers And Declarations in the Courts of Heaven For Victory, Breakthrough, and Deliverance

37.   How to make the Holy Ghost Your Closest Friend (Book 2)

Pius Joseph

Witchcraft Summons

95

98

99

Pius Joseph

Witchcraft Summons

Pius Joseph

www.ingramcontent.com/pod-product-compliance
Lightning Source LLC
Chambersburg PA
CBHW061324120726
48001CB00002B/673